POEMS YOU MAY
HAVE MISSED

POEMS YOU MAY HAVE MISSED

Selected by

BARRY FANTONI

GOMPERS PRESS

This edition first published in Great Britain in 2021 by Gompers Press, London

Gompers Press
3 Franconia Road, London SW4 9NB

ISBN 978 1 73991 47 0 7

British Library Cataloguing-in-Publication Data
A catalogue record for this book is available on request from the British Library.

Edited by Alison Rae
Designed and typeset by Teresa Monachino

Printed and bound by T J Books Limited, Padstow, UK

To Barry Ernest Booth

CONTENTS

INTRODUCTION

For over fifty years Edith Gryce edited the *Toronto Poetry Forum*. It was published quarterly and had a small but appreciative readership throughout Canada. I met her at an international poetry festival, to which I had been invited to read poetry by *Private Eye*'s E. J. Thribb.

When Edith died in 2016 her devoted companion Dorothy Bellingham was tasked with sorting her affairs. On clearing out an old filing cabinet, an unmarked folder containing over a hundred poems was found. Some were neatly typed. Others were scribbled on scraps of paper and cigarette packets.

Although not an expert, Dorothy instantly recognised the names of T. S. Eliot, Sylvia Plath and Pam Ayres, among others. Hoping that I might shed some light on the matter, Dorothy sent the poems to me.

While many were clearly authentic, the canto by Ezra Pound for example, others appeared to be little short of outright parodies. Gerard Manley Hopkins' poem 'Out of a Job' has an oblique reference to *The Third Man*, a film made fifty years after his death. Unless he had been given powers to see into the future, 'Out of a Job' must have been written by another hand. But whose? With Edith no longer able to explain how she came by this uncommon collection of verse, we can only guess as to its origins.

From the poems that Dorothy sent me, I have selected those I enjoyed reading most – purely for my pleasure and nothing else. I set aside the matter of authenticity when choosing the poems in this collection and hope you will do the same.

ANNA AKHMATOVA

Fragment

(10 December 1913, Tashkent)

The dark hills and black
Winter are
Sleeping on my heart—

Only the pine forests and skies
Of my childhood comfort me . . .

Soon I shall escape
This timeless isolation . . .

Translated by Natalia Slivorska.

SIMON ARMITAGE

Self Portrait

Not quite Ted Hughes,
As much as I enthuse.

Nor Homer, come to think of it,
Although I did my bit.

Nor am I a W. H. Auden.
Right. So, that's that, then.

(*Editor's note*: The chord symbols G, F and C are scribbled in pencil
above some of the words.)

PAM AYRES

Ayers Rock

Ooh, it is such fun to be alive,
Because you never know what's next.
News arrives all unexpected,
Like when someone sends a text.

Well, the other day I read
There is a rock down under,
And they named it after me.
A sort of world's ninth wonder.

Ayers Rock, goodness, what an honour!
And it's *such* a massive size.
You know, my dears, it's almost like
I've won the Pulitzer Prize.

GEORGE BARKER

Street Ballad

Pretty little girl
    ate pie and mash.
She paid with smiles—
    she had no cash.

JOHN BETJEMAN
Dear John

Here comes summer, here comes sun,
Here comes lots of outdoor fun.
Up the river, in a punt,
Glimpsing Gilly Gilkes's ~~cunt~~. cleavage.

Tea and scones upon the grass,
Hasn't she a lovely ~~arse?~~ smile?
Look, my tea is full of ants,
There's something stirring in my ~~pants. loins.~~ cup.

Now it's winter, snow is falling,
I've got some news that's quite appalling.
Poor old poet's 'bout to blub,
Gilly Gilkes ~~is in the club.~~ has got a job at Harvey Nicks.

(*Editor's note*: The following instruction was added to the foot
of the poem: <u>Be a dear and sort it out.</u>)

ELIZABETH BISHOP

The Baker of Pedra Azul 4 p.m.
(Rio de Janeiro)

… infinite patience and diligence
　　　　—Vasari's *Lives of the Artists*

For Mr. Howard Clamberg & Mr. Gilbert Hosebeam

It's hot by the oven
baking bread and those
tasty *pains au chocolat* they eat
in this quaint old village
—or was that Paris?—
so he does not mind too much
rising every morning
including Sundays and Christmas
as the sun also rises,

because at that time of day
the air is cool and he can
roll out the dough, as if they
were tiny carpets on his marble
table, and not perspire
as he will later when the sun
climbs over the church of
San Salvador,

at five his wife will rise
and help him by feeding wood
picked from starved hills
into the mouth of the oven;
and while the bread bakes
he will stand watching her—
admiring the way her dark hair
dances as she moves,
and how her laughter is
like the sound of gold rain,
and he is never more contented.

WILLIAM BLAKE

Southend-on-Sea

I amble on the mile-long pier,
As did our Lord the waves once tread.
Here to order flasks of beer,
In every pint a sorrow shed.

The mussel, whelk and scuttling crab,
No harm they ever did.
Nor fish 'pon fresh fishmonger's slab:
Cod, plaice and common squid.

Each shrimp in every shrimping net,
Grants cruelty a number.
A boiling pot feels no regret,
For shrimps' eternal slumber.

(*Editor's note*: I suspect there were more verses, but all I could find
were etchings of pie and mash shops and stalls selling sand buckets.)

ELIZABETH BARRETT BROWNING

A Woman's Love

This aching heart, grief in all but name,
Hangs as the winter branch snow bedecked;
A frozen sadness that would see in spring
Pears and almonds but for this winter-long
Measure of dark sorrow, once born in me
As purest laughter, like the silver waters
Of an endless brook—dead now, love
Lost as colours in winter's flower gardens,
Now and for ever and eternity.

Death thou art cunning to set out love
As satin soft and honey sweet to
Cheat this lover weeping at your feet.

ROBERT BROWNING
Give Me Tuscany Any Day

Look; there's no point in beating about
The bush. We are all going to die
Sooner or later, and if you listen
To Mrs Browning it is more likely to be
Sooner—tomorrow, or God forbid
this evening, suddenly—out of the blue!
Anyway, that's neither here nor there.
My point is that since we are all bound
For the big sleep so to speak, we might
As well live somewhere truly splendid
And make the most of it while we are
Still wrapped in our mortal coil—as
Hamlet once put it; a corner of
God's creation that does his divine
handiwork full justice. I am talking
About Tuscany—old Etrusca; the land
Those thick-headed Romans sacked back
In seven hundred BC. Take my word for it,
There's no place on earth to compare.
Tuscany's got it all: art, sensational views,
Old barns ripe for conversion. So—
Okay, the white wines are not as varied
As you might find, say, in the Loire Valley,
But for my money there's nothing to beat
A full-blooded Chianti Classico. No wonder
They call Tuscany the Bordeaux of Italy.

You can keep your overpriced Monte Carlo—
Give me Tuscany any day.

Note to self: Must drop dear Fannie a card.

CHARLES BUKOWSKI

Wrong Number

at the door clutching
a rain-soaked card
with a number in running
ink scribbled on the back

are you Stockman? she says
I tell her that's me
in all those screwed-up paper
balls around the trash can.

an hour later I roll off her
you fuck like a whore, I say,
and fuck her again

I smoke a cigarette
while she dresses and colours
her lips cherry apple red
who's Stockman? I ask

she drops the wax stick back
in her purse and snaps it shut.

Nobody, she says.
Nobody I ever met.

C. P. CAVAFY

Waiting in the Taverna

He sat there in the corner of the taverna,
Thinking as he always did about the afternoon.
Of those rotten hours stolen in a rented room.

He was waiting for him, the boy with the scarf
worn like a noose, with eyes that looked but
never greeted him. Who spoke only in numbers.

Here was the sadness that never left him,
Sorrow for which no love could offer consolation.

Translated by Philip Conner.

JOHN CLARE

The Miller's Song

I love thee, gentle Mary
    From the dairy.
Love I thy pale fair skin,
    More white than milk put
In a churn, for sight of it,
    My heart doth burn.

I love thee, gentle Mary
    From the dairy.
All day I brood, at night
    I pine.
For longing, dear,
    To call thee mine.

I love thee, gentle Mary
    From the dairy.
Love thee as the cow loves grass,
    As pollen loves the bee.
I love thee, gentle Mary,
    Dost thou, Mary, lovest me?

JOHN COOPER CLARKE

Rambling Man

I once worked in Salford Tech,
A rope around my fucking neck.

(*Editor's note*: I cut the preceding 32 couplets and the 58 that followed.
They read as somewhat repetitive.)

WENDY COPE

A Gentleman's Word

A gentleman once told me, my love,
Your eyes are bluer than a summer's sky,
Your nature sweeter than an apple pie.

A gentleman once told me, my heart,
Your skin is softer than a velvet glove,
Your voice coos like a turtle dove.

A gentleman once told me, my desire,
Your smile would melt a heart of ice,
Its value is beyond all price.

A gentleman once told me, my precious,
Share my bed and share my life,
Tomorrow you will be my wife.

Dressed in my wedding trousseau white,
I waited all day at the altar,
Without a gentleman in sight.

the world is full of liv-ing parts
of which the human race is o n e.Some)
have been here from
the s tart & some; have just be gun
relatively (s-Peking)—most survive
pretty well all things considered while
others fall at the first fence (1th) eg

:old brachiosaurus- a few
make this old wOrLD a place to grace) (bees
termites trout.   i'm thinking bout– but(
not man(– a half descent chap he-thinks
imself who t,u,r,n,s out to be a sort
of two bit Phoney chimpanzeE minus
charm) yepp ... (charm

weez a dis-eased sap says i (some WHATunkindly
.yet   in all our daysfilled mitt two leg struttin
mister man has master minded nuttin
=worth a word of prAise.all pleas(e) stop
the rot(homo sapiens Gott started mankind
ruthlessly goes on his way m.a.d/ goaded
(no can do_ bud
is still as more or less the total SiZ-E of al' his;
    (will) sighs me

DANTE
Inferno

Where the hell am I?

Translated by Raymond Jarre.

(*Editor's note*: This is possibly an early draft.)

EMILY DICKINSON

3,975

Dead Finch from Flight—
he sings
Silently of Love—

Wings long lost
Returned seen—
In His Celestial Light—

CAROL ANN DUFFY

Another Moon

Silver shards from another moon
slide through slits in the blind.

They lightly bond our burning bodies,
cut painlessly across our skin.

My fingers tip-tiptoe eagerly towards
your tight moonlit nipples.

I taste crispy salt on your wet lips.
You kiss me through ripples of tears.

You take my whispered order to love you
as a waiter with too many to serve.

At dawn, I wake to find you gone.
At dusk, you come back as the scent of musk.

T. S. ELIOT

The Waste Bin

Ibi non sit allies

(*Editor's note*: No poem accompanied the above epigraph, only the following textual notes.)

The Waste Bin

1. The Latin text of the epigraph is an improvised aside by the comic performer Maximilian Molinarius (63 BC).
2. Line 7. Cf. *Galacticus* II, iv.
3. Ibid. VI, viii.
53. The ancient Chinese word game of Ying Tong, from which much of this section of the poem is borrowed (5–106).
55. Jacobo Tovaliogli makes a brief appearance in Lassparri's 18th-century comic opera, *Gottlieb auf Naxo*.
107. A Heal's desk lamp.
115. Young's Medical Manual, 1899. Vol. 1, ch. xxi: Imido tetramethyl diamido diphenyl methane hydrochlorate merck; apyonine: c. p. auramine.
123. The view from my office window at 24 Russell Square.
125. Cf. Vincent the Poor, *Confessions*, p. 872.
126. Ibid.
130. Cf. The Rome Express (Southbound): '*É vietato sputare in carrozze di prima classe.*'
167. The telephone number of Lady Ottoline Morrell's London residence. Mrs Cravat is her housekeeper.
169. Deutrement's *La Brousse Lavande Oublié* I, ii.
170. Ibid.
171. Qv.
172. Cf. Henri de Mougins, *Isabella*, vol. 6, ch. vi, note to Blackmans, printers of the English edition (1879): 'Dear Sirs, Please check the spelling.'
180. 'Oompah, oompah, stick it up your joompah' (anon.).
202. *The New Home Encyclopaedia* (Bassett & Pink, Idaho, 1907).
203. *Midgley's Quotes & Quotations* (Peedle Press, 1903).
204. *A Guide to India* (Chandra, Wheatly & Vetch, 1813).
227. The Golden Bough Curry House, Bloomsbury, September 12th, 1919. One Tikka Masala, 1s 3d. One Brinjal Bhaji, 6d. One Chapati, 2d. One Lassi, 1d. Total excluding service. 2s 3d.
228. Drop G. F. a note about expenses.

ROBERT FROST
Salt and Pepper

Two pots on table cloth await,
Cooked food served on a china plate.
Each seasoning to give back taste,
To goodness lost and thought as waste.

ALLEN GINSBERG

Wandering

In the Dharma Bar
Cyd Charisse danced
her long legs plenty
Sirimavo Bandaranaike
gave a speech about
her new political party
Liberace sang
Beale Street Blues
sadly out of key
Rock Hudson
smiled Hollywood
lovely lips
in my direction
then to requests
I recited 'Howl'
and took a bow
around four
I stepped out
into a pale sun
rising in a misty
city dawn light
to find my MOTHER
Naomi is standing
right there naked
on the sidewalk
mad at me as ever

shave that beard
she is saying Allen
you look like
a redneck from
the Ozarks
marry a nice
Jewish girl
settle down
bring up a family
don't go crazy like
your father and me
quit hanging around
with all those beats
and fruits listen
to your mother
Allen baby for just one
time in your life
forget Walt Whitman
—be a *mensch*.

Berkeley, March, 1956

(*Editor's note*: There are five preceding pages of this poem.
Lack of space prevents their inclusion here.)

ROBERT GRAVES

Poppy Red

Poppy red my true love's lips,
Her eyes are opals, heart of gold.
Into my dreams each night she trips,
To tell me love will not grow cold.

Snow white her skin, yet warm as stones
That slumber in the summer sun.
She weeps to hear the dying groans,
Of lives lived out, yet scarce begun.

Poppy red my true love's lips,
As red as any soldier's blood.
From wounds my future slowly drips,
And turns French fields to graves of mud.

TONY HARRISON
The Ballad of Old Bothy

It seems t'were only yesterday
when I were just a lad,
when much that gave us cause to pray
were less than what we had.

But there were always jam for bread
and gravy for our peas,
boots had soles, sheets covered bed,
and everyone said please.

From dawn to dusk Mam mopped floor
to keep our house a palace.
The brass on't step of our front door
gleamed brighter than church chalice.

God bless Mam's fear of mortal sin
and bless her artful thrift.
The mites she saved in't biscuit tin
gave us our Christmas gift.

Our dad baked bread to earn a crust,
and being truly humble,
even midst the flour and yeast
I never heard him grumble.

I knew a life of baking bread
were never to be mine.
I wanted to tread a road well read,
and know how words got to rhyme.

So leaving school in '53,
I didn't throw me cap in.
I went to Leeds's university,
to study Greek and Latin.

[*Editor's note*: According to the page numbers,
possibly thirty verses appear to be missing at
this point.]

Now I am three score and ten
and maybe just a few years more.
I often dream of my life then;
the Classics never were a chore.

When on the up-line train from Leeds,
it passes Bothwell Park.
I gaze at benches, swings and trees,
us names carved on their bark.

Behind bushes in dead of night
young Willie found his Fanny.
Cocks were aimed without a sight,
their accuracy uncanny.

There, manhood kissed a lass's lips.
There, sticky seeds were scattered.
There, BOYS were MEN with filter tips.
There, young men's dreams were shattered.

But parks pay Tory council's wage.
Tomorrow they will come.
Build luxury homes on heritage.
THE FUCKING BLOODY SUCKING SCUM.

The bankers and the marketeer
will occupy our land.
Old Bothy Park will disappear,
like piss does in't sand.

SEAMUS HEANEY

Bogged Down

I could just make out my father
Through the ill-fitting weather-
Worn door's wood slats filtering
Thin strips of stubble land
Light to the damp dank dark bog
Where I sat daily.

This side of the demesne wall,
Between scattered bullaun, tall,
Unmovable as the violet-pillowed
Mountains shielding Mossbawn,
My father's vast frame cast
A shadow wider than Tievebulliagh.

That morning, as one distracted
By the crack-throated call of unsold
Cattle (or a distant croppie's instant
Song), my father turned his head to face
Heaven, and saw so much there
He, as I, so little understood.

GEORGE HERBERT

Transformation

How rich becomes God's
    Earthly store
When man seeketh wealth
    In humble chore.

Thus, in a heart transformed,
    God's love to measure:
Our drudgeries
    Become life's treasure.

GERARD MANLEY HOPKINS

Out of a Job

Bed-sheet-strewn tea-cold toast rushed from fasting break-
made table tumbles tussled
down the tube, where to discover,
no Camden train to town untunnell'd rumbles.

O, unblesséd underground!
Gold as Golders Green-gilled gold as gold unseen between
your iron lines I find,
I have arrived too late.

Dismissed for sin of tardiness;
the greater justice greater less when dappled
wings can fly while I can all but crawl!

Life now is a buckled timeness filled to pass
the days unpaid, in Odeons I creep, to sit
fitfully, eyes glazed, half asleep.

From penny pews I view the Pathé news,
then main-featured Holly Martins meeting
in a man-made trinity; dark Wells
talks 'old man' of human hells and Swiss-made
cuckoo clocks that hang along a Harry Lime.

HORACE

Ode V.1

Greetings, Kyriad, most noble Nivean, who
took my yoke and suffered long the wit of
      unshaved Anandin—
      tell me news of your days in Meltus.
      Of blushing Enos pouring wines from Moorish skins.

Venos wept while tall nocturnal pines
held back his sorrows from the moon—
      Recall you, Priton—
      like Nytol here stilled ill-fated
      in his untamed dreams.

We shall speak no more of war and waste in
Melton's mallow marshes. We are weary of winter,
      her fated harvest gripped in ice—
      Mensa's anguish hardens as a marble robe,
      his olive trees anticipate the august dawn.

Translated by Dr Gilbert Jebb.

A. E. HOUSMAN

While Still a Lad

While still a lad, he knew by heart
When seasons came and seasons went.
He knew the day when spring would start,
And snow the slender branches bent.

The lad called love, and found it rare,
In his own form did love reply,
No buxom lass was waiting there,
But love outlawed, love to deny.

In Breddon Jail the lad awaits,
His love will meet no clemency.
A mob is waiting at the gates,
Pointing to the hangman's tree.

TED HUGHES

Crow

High in the lupin sky, a crow crows, soars,
A torn-throated vole caged in her clinging
Claws. Each destiny is like a universal
Epitaph—to bone and dust it moves us all.

The sty gate open; spilled blood wall.
Drawn bolts oiled with slaughter creak.
He saunters forth, crooning my name as a
Mate of Judas might, offering me trite
Assurances to deflect his murderous mission.

Cloven-footed family friend, to fated
Fetid fat-stripped blood-bleached bacon.
Yon son of a cutthroat farmer sent to
Do God's will. His will be done. Pig's will.

CLIVE JAMES
Dropping a Line

Mart's just called me from *The Spectator*
To fix up lunch at the *Ivy* for one or later.
Then *Harold's* dropping by at four,
And it's off to see Pete's *new Bernard Shaw*.
It's *The Apple Cart*, with *Dame J. Dench*
As *Orinthia*, the King's delicious wench.
Mrs Patrick Campbell starred in the first production,
Playing with great skill the art of seduction.

(*Editor's note*: There are 58 more verses of this poem.
Lack of space prevents their inclusion here.)

RUDYARD KIPLING
Exceedingly Good

Cakes-cakes-cakes-cakes-

(*Editor's note*: This short line was scribbled in pencil on the back of a
packet of Passing Cloud cigarettes.)

PHILIP LARKIN

Hard Times

It's hard to find someone to fuck,
The last I had was down to luck.
She works with me in the library,
Stamping books and making tea.

In my bedsit, drinking Ovaltine,
I played Bunk Johnson in between
Rubbing her tits to get her randy
And making sure I had some Durex handy.

It wasn't what you'd call a spree,
The fault was largely down to me.
I'm bald, myopic, dull and lank,
And just as happy with a wank.

AMY LOWELL

Not All There

You enter softer than a sigh.
Brighter than all heaven's stars
Set in her velvet sky!

Perfume of night jasmine
Disturbs this undressed dream.
A reverie forever here
To sew the unstitched seam.

Your mouth filled with summer.
Your lips red as rosehips.
Ripe fruit of autumn's dawn,
You are mine to pluck and relish!

ROBERT LOWELL

Dr Gachet

A little longer, Doctor; I paint from that vacant
stupor given in the sleepy haze of afternoon,
my concern falling just short of the listener,
like a dart that doesn't reach the board—
the way a priest nods in the stricken face
of confessed pain and penitence . . . Done; there,
your flat fingers pointing to the vase of foxglove,
the captain's hat now too heavy on your brow . . .
An elbow bent at books written by two brothers
you will read one day when you have less pressing
issues—the mad . . . the incurable mad
screaming to be loved, to be heard in their
dark cells: the glass of white Chablis waiting
impatiently beside a plate of cold meats.

ROGER McGOUGH

Shoe Business

Last week
I bought a pair
of new shoes.

I'm wearing them in
so I don't
wear them out.

MARIANNE MOORE

To a Front-loading Washer

Watching
washing spin, the spin I'm in,
wishing I was washing
not watching, cleansed-in-the-oval lens
looking like an open oven
roasting turkey not my
ignominious lingerie tangling with a pair
of Y-fronts briefly before
encountering
my *broderie anglaise* bra purchased
    —should there be the taking of notes—
not in Alabama, mutton-head
                but! This instead;
be alerted, *Monsieur*, I am easily affronted
by jesty questions when you know full well
                that I opine
bons mots are more my line, some say
mine are divine—dined out on quite a few
ones old and new—that's my girl—integral,
on and on the soap suds swirl,
round and round making slappy-sloppy sounds,
go quick, go slow, go fast, until at last
the ten-cent cycle ceases (think of pressing
all those creases)
                when

washing-clean and washing-fresh
demands no more

>for watching washing is a little thought
>made large through much excess.

PAUL MULDOON
The Saints Preserve Us

If youse ever go across the sea to
Keenaghan bejesus youse are sure to find
some fine potato pickin' there,
    begorrah, when Irish eyes
are smilin' it's a long way to Tipperary.

All you fine lads, Liam, Sean and Declan,
let's down to the village for a pint,
get some in and get locked up for the night.

Put down your picks and pick up a ticket,
there's a boat leavin' for New York town,
the Bronx is up and the Bowery down.

All you fine lads,
let's dig a canal, then brew some *poitín*
in Padraig's old pail,

the one he got from his brave granda
who got himself shot in the IRA.

SYLVIA PLATH

Reflux

The hissing skillet
Flames bacon crisp
As a martyr's skin

Acid leaks into
This peeled pink shrimp
The coiled snake, a raw

Nettle belly well
Filling with swill
Of jellied eels

Birds singing
Without a throat,
Their song echoes

In the jellyfish
Flesh of the
Swollen knee so

Easily mistaken for
A dead child's
Head.

EZRA POUND

Canto CXVIV

Y'd be nuts too!"
Sitting in the tap room *di baggio Firenze*
Sending Tom them clauses you cut."

F&F to E. Z. *passim*
Not withstanding. Not with. The pact signed by
Sultan Mohammad Khudabanda (Mr. to most)
&
Them boys from YONDER
An ol' Brig. Gen. Leonard Covington
(Fatally wounded at the Battle of Beach Farm)

1813
ϖιάσει ένα αστέρι ϖου ϖέφτει
Jus' look how done took all them IDEAS
You gave him an' all them   notions"
For turning @
rags   ράκη
into SILKS
An' him a YANK same as you and him putting
IN all them Greek words and Latin doohickeys
To spice it up.
Not to mention Chinaman talk."
Wang Bang Dang

Inky Pinky Parlez Vous

....

On his death bed
Marco Polo said
Good night Irene.

                              CACOETHES SCRIBENDI
To the Captain of the *Saucy Lady*.
Order fresh water for the pigs and goats."

                                    Girart de Montcorbier. 1455.

    (and the g'd for nothing Comte von Hopp)
Taking a mouthful of Sol's cherry cheesecake . . .
:USERY

LXV   Old Tom got away with it and you went nuts."
       C'd not tell Sweeney from a jar of pickled eggs."
       CANTO CANTAS CANTAT
       Ain't that just the end?"

LAURA RIDING

Nil Desperandum

We are not getting any younger.
Me the rotten half-eaten apple rotting,
You the soiled seeds spilled on the spoiled
Earth—the dearth of reptilian love
Delivered like a dead letter in the kiss
Placed on my sun-blistered lips
Neglected: that night we slept
Naked in the late slave trader's ditch
Then in the morning we hitched a lift
From Wyoming to Galveston, New Mexico.
Why Wyoming? Ming the Chinese tractor
Driver laughed and his gold teeth
Glinted like nuggets in the sun,
And I knew we were grieving for ourselves
In that rain-soaked shelter,
Or was it that diner in South Carolina
Where we made our open confession
Of mediocre ability spoken as a token.
And yet we keep on going . . .

RAINER MARIA RILKE

Marionette

He dangles there; suspended from his
infinite hook, on invisible wires which
you will not see when he performs,
cavorting on indifferent wooden limbs
in the ineluctable hands of his master.

The marionette's tethered fate decreed
sightless, his world unseen in painted eyes,
a timeless grin to register his sap-dry
history pitted against the overwhelming
future that is broken stillness.

For it is we who will ultimately
determine who dances and who is dead;
higher forces themselves are subject
to the parade of chance, the inexhaustible
possibilities suspended in thin air.

Translated by Eric Stephens.

CHRISTINA ROSSETTI

A Fold That Has No Lamb

A fold that has no lamb
      Is a heart shorn of love,
An empty space more sadder than
      The loveless soul I am.

SAINT JOHN OF THE CROSS

XXIII

Dark Rapture

In hearts of human love,
Redeemed from darkest night,
In daytime now received,
God's everlasting light.

Translated by Felix Field.

STEVIE SMITH

Grave Concerns

If life is a path
From our birth
To our death,
On which I wander
With shortening breath,
What is it for?
This I frequently ponder.

STEPHEN SPENDER
On the Fourth Day

On the fourth summer day I entered a room
Abandoned and rootless without roots
Silence lost in celestial skin-lit roots
And the snow-white walls celestial because
Celestial is a word that is transpierced
With longer and less accessible words
Not sure where this is going but a forest
Might be good in a once-marooned field
Of stars splintered falling like ice-
Filled moonbeams on rootless dreams of
Man-made injustice heaped on the dying
Being that way inclined politically
Red to my roots time now to move on to
All the famous people I have met.
T. S. Eliot who discovered me.
W. H. Auden was at the same school in Holt.
Ernest Hemingway whom I met in Spain and Paris.
Dylan Thomas. W. B. Yeats. Jean-Paul Sartre.
Louis MacNeice.
Virginia Woolf. Isaiah Berlin.
Roy Campbell. Colin Wilson. Raymond Chandler.
Ted Hughes (a tad serious).
Cecil Day-Lewis.
Then there are the painters.
Picasso. Moore. Arp …
The list is endless …

WALLACE STEVENS

Ten Ways to Oven-bake a Ukulele

1

Seek outsized moonbeams,
Go get a yellow swan,
Then move to South Dakota.

2

O rock of Yakahuladikydula,
The shadow of hungry washboards,
My mailman delivered three ripe cherries.

3

Hot dogs and candy-pink roses,
These are the orchids of the night,
My boots belongs to Daddy.

(*Editor's note*: The remaining seven verses appear to be missing.)

DYLAN THOMAS

Epilogue

Dominions lost, this late
Prince of Wales outcast,
D.T.s D.T.s, detected,
Ruffled duffle-coated
Ale a hopping pub a-picking
A standing man a-falling
Out from oak-wood beer,
A pouring drunk in lyrics,
Licked like lollies, sick as dogs,
From no hope to no anchor barred,
Never more the till bell chiming,
Hard on pavement body falls in
Rain-soaked early sodden dawn.

Timble-tumble out from coach
And yawning headlong horses
Naggering, braggering, staggering,
Oh, kingdoms lost for metre's sake
Repetition reputations make, choirs
Of coal black black as coal black
White as coal white black as
White coal black as angels white
As coal black white as milk
Shakes a-singing, *Another Little
Drink Won't Do You Any Harm.*
Bitter downed, better drowned,

Fishwives get a mention on a farm
For reason's gone and gone
For reason mine's a lager large one,
Boyo, my darling Clementine,
Gone forever numberless fish boxes
Shoeless, sockless, topless,
Just a chaser then, your shout!

Waking, warbled, garbled,
Latch of key in open quietly door,
Stairs to climb into the womb
I call my rented ten-bob room
My horsehair tomb is empty,
Alas no lass, no milk-white breasts,
No proud crow's nest to kiss
Undressed between a soft caress
An underlaying sleepless
Filth-filled sheets to shroud;
A candle flickers at his head;
Into his bed the verse-cursed
Welsh-made maker tumbling,
Mumbling God, who is to judge
This versing man, for all his sins
Made worse?

DEREK WALCOTT

Nomorus

Lovely ladies and kind sirs,
welcome to Nomorus, our island in the sun,
where my people have toiled

since time began. Tho' I may sail on many a sea,
her shores will always be home to me.
It all looks five-star comfort now,

happy holidaymakers, but our
history has been long and painful.
We were once slaves, sweating

under the yoke of evil colonialism,
a time when slaves were treated
no better than slaves.

Our tribe was a chained and bloody line
of men, women and children, slaves
beaten into tending the burnt remains

of freedom our masters heaped
upon our cherished golden beaches.
But thankfully that was long ago,

and today we have grown rich on
bananas, yams and tinned peaches.
And hotels!

Most have two swimming pools (one with swim-up pool bar),
beach grill, three floodlit tennis courts,
scuba diving, jacuzzi bath tub, piano bar,

Hobie Cat sailing, snorkelling, golf,
a hairdryer in every room and
glass-bottom boat tours.

Hector came, so did Archimedes,
Artemis, Demeter, Castor, Nestor.
Or they didn't.

Oh, island in the sun, willed to me by my father's hand.
All my days I will sing in praise
of your forest waters, your shining sand.

Hello, lovely young lady.
Let me show you around.

WALT WHITMAN
Song of Myself LIII

I am the prodigal song of all passion.
I am all words sung sweet from bliss-filled
Lips. I am my song. Mine alone.
Woke up this mornin' at the crow of the cock
And took myself over to see
Old Hank Jeffers at his dry feed store.
There ain't nothing you can tell Hank about
Trout fishing; he knows a spot down by
Hibbard's Creek, where the wood ducks are seen
Soaring at dusk, and where the red woman lives
Alone—hang'st thou on, pardner.
What's that young wan-faced boy doing with his
Pants around his ankles? His naked torso
Glistening wet in the noonday sun. Swimming
Naked, I will wager a mule to a bale of hay.
I best go'st see. For maybe he will become
Eventually the great gatherer of my
Man Woman Man soul. Lordy, Lordy! Lord!
Lay thee beside me, now, here, sweet chil' of
Love-tossed dreams, lay thy body here 'pon the
Dew-damp leaves and grass.
Forget the goddamn ants.

W. B. YEATS

I Met Love's Dance

Young limbs in love, you danced your days;
Dissembled man, I was awoken.
Leaping then, an eager Actaeon. Hades
hid in fear, for lust I was outspoken
    By the old stone wall.

Now a bone man at his beer; dismembered
Loins recall our daily prance.
Bitter now, the fragrant taste remembered
Youth undressed for love's sweet dalliance
    By the old stone wall.

Bent-framed, one weary limb the other follows;
On fresh turned earth, lying side by side
Two granite flags cover lightless hollows;
One marks the groom, one love's dancing bride
    By the old stone wall.

BIOGRAPHICAL
NOTES

ANNA AKHMATOVA was born in Bol'shoi Fontan, near Odessa in 1889. Her first husband, the poet Nikolay Gumilev, was executed by Soviet secret police in 1921. Her common-law husband, Nikolay Punin, and her son, Lev, were condemned to the gulag. Punin died in a camp in 1953. Akhmatova had many lovers, including the poet Osip Mandelstam, who was also sent to a gulag to die. On a visit to Paris she had a passionate affair with Modigliani. During the Siege of Leningrad in radio broadcasts, she read wounded soldiers her verses, which she had learned by heart, as poetry books not authorised by the state were burned. She died in 1966 after a heart attack and was buried in Komarovo.

SIMON ARMITAGE was born in West Yorkshire in 1963, and lives there today. He studied geography at Portsmouth University and did a postgraduate course at Manchester University. Without a job, Simon followed in his father's footsteps and became a probation officer. His father is well known for writing pantos for the local amateur dramatic society in the village of Marsden, where Simon grew up. In 2019, Simon was appointed UK Poet Laureate. He is the lead singer of The Scaremongers, who have 35 monthly listeners on Spotify.

PAM AYRES was born in Stanford in the Vale in 1947. After a stint in the Women's Royal Air Force she made her name by appearing on the popular TV talent show, *Opportunity Knocks*. Numerous TV appearances followed, and Pam became a much-loved entertainer. She divides the critics: some say she is a charming faux-naïf; others, less kindly, call her work childish drivel.

Either way, she has sold many millions of books, albums, CDs and DVDs, her books have been in the *Sunday Times* bestseller charts in (almost) every decade since the seventies, and she is New Zealand's favourite poet. Pam was awarded the MBE in the Queen's Birthday Honours of 2004.

GEORGE BARKER was born in 1913, in Loughton, Essex. He went to Regent Street Polytechnic, where he read English. While on a visit to the USA, he met Elizabeth Smart, famous for her novel *By Grand Central Station I Sat Down And Wept*, an account of their affair. Barker wrote nineteen books of poetry and fathered fifteen children – four with Smart. At one point, he wrote porn for Anaïs Nin. He died in Norfolk in 1991.

SIR JOHN BETJEMAN was born in Camden, London, in 1906. After school, where he was taught by T. S. Eliot, he went to Magdalen College, Oxford. Owing to his lack of interest (C. S. Lewis called him an idle prig), he left without a degree. Described by some as 'temperamentally gay', in 1933 Sir John married the Hon. Penelope Chetwode, the only daughter of Field Marshal Philip Walhouse Chetwode, 1st Baron Chetwode, 7th Baronet of Oakley, GCB, OM, GCSI, KCMG, DSO, and fathered two children. After Penelope became a devout Roman Catholic the couple drifted apart. Sir John then met Lady Elizabeth Cavendish, daughter of the 10th Duke of Devonshire and a lady-in-waiting to Princess Margaret for six decades. He was UK Poet Laureate from 1972 until his peaceful death at home in Trebetherick, Cornwall, in 1984. Elizabeth was by his side.

ELIZABETH BISHOP was born in Worcester, Massachusetts, in 1911. Her exceptionally wealthy father died when she was eight months old and her mother was committed to a mental asylum when she was five. Elizabeth was a sickly child and remained in ill health throughout her life, which she spent mostly travelling around the world. She was an alcoholic who once described herself as the loneliest person who ever lived. She wrote 101 poems in her lifetime. Bishop won the Pulitzer Prize for poetry in 1956, and she was the first American and the first woman to be awarded the Neustadt International Prize for Literature in 1976. She died of a cerebral aneurysm at her home in Boston in 1979.

WILLIAM BLAKE was born in 1757, in what is now London's Soho. He had a happy childhood, one largely spent avoiding school. Throughout his life, Blake was prone to having visions. As a four-year-old he saw God. He frequently encountered angels, and once glimpsed Satan standing at the bottom of his staircase. Blake taught himself Greek, Latin, Hebrew and Italian to get a better understanding of the Bible. On the one hand, he was extremely religious, believing Jesus to be the link between God and Man, and on the other, a radical political thinker, profoundly affected by the French Revolution. As well as writing countless poems on God and democracy, Blake worked as a journeyman engraver to earn money. When he married Catherine Boucher, his wife could not read or write; he taught her to do both, and showed her how to colour his vast output of etchings. Blake is perhaps best known for his epic poem, 'Jerusalem'. He died singing a hymn in 1827.

ELIZABETH BARRETT BROWNING was born in Kelloe, County Durham, in 1806, the first of eleven siblings. Her family owned sugar plantations in Jamaica and a large fleet of cargo ships. A studious child, before the age of twelve she had read English, Greek and Roman history, chunks of Shakespeare and *Paradise Lost*, plays by Racine and Molière, and works by Rousseau and Voltaire – many of them in the original language. In her youth, she would be considered one of England's greatest living poets. She was a passionate supporter of Mary Wollstonecraft and, despite her family's business interests, opposed to slavery and child labour. When she was fifteen, Elizabeth suffered a spinal injury, and later fell sick with a lung disorder. Opium was used as a treatment, but it did not help, and she remained a semi-invalid for the rest of her life. Aged forty, Elizabeth married Robert Browning in secret. She was promptly disinherited by her father, and the couple moved to Italy where their son, Pen, was born. Elizabeth died in Florence in 1861, in her husband's arms, uttering the word 'beautiful'.

ROBERT BROWNING was born in Camberwell, London, in 1812. His father worked as a clerk for the Bank of England and was an avid book collector. His mother was a talented musician. Robert's was a loving, supportive family. By the age of fourteen, he was fluent in French, Italian, Greek and Latin. He was a vegetarian and, probably, an atheist, and lived at home until he married Elizabeth Barrett in 1846. It was a happy marriage. Robert's voice can be heard on a wax cylinder recording made by an artist friend at a dinner party in 1889. He died at his son's home in Venice after catching a cold the same year.

CHARLES BUKOWSKI was born Heinrich Karl Bukowski in 1920, in Andernach, Germany. His father was a sergeant in the US Army who married a local girl. A month after Charles was born, they sailed to the States. Bukowski grew up in Los Angeles, a skinny kid with bad skin who was bullied by classmates and his father. He started drinking and smoking heavily from a very early age and failed his army medical owing to his addiction to alcohol. He worked first in a pickle factory and then for the US Post Office. In 1957, he married Barbara Frye, a poetry editor from Texas. The marriage lasted two years. She died in mysterious circumstances in India. In 1985, he married Linda Lee Beighle, who ran a health-food restaurant and had inherited a fortune. The service was conducted by a Canadian mystic. Bukowski's books were widely translated and sold in millions. The FBI is known to have kept a file on him in 1968. His last work, completed just before his death from leukaemia in 1994, with Linda by his side, was *Pulp*.

CONSTANTINE P. CAVAFY was born in Alexandria, Egypt, in 1862. As a teenager, he lived in Liverpool. After returning to Alexandria, he worked as a clerk in the Ministry of Public Works. Early on, instead of looking for a publisher, he would just make copies of his poems and give them to his friends. They were often sexually explicit, describing fleeting homosexual encounters. He wrote his major works after he turned forty. Cavafy is thought to be one of the greatest Greek poets of the twentieth century. He died from lung cancer on his seventieth birthday.

JOHN CLARE was born in Helpston, Northamptonshire, in 1793. His father was a farm labourer. When John was a child, he saw a loader slip from a wagon and break his neck. The trauma is thought to have been responsible for Clare's chronic mental illness. Aged sixteen, he fell passionately in love with Mary Joyce, but her wealthy father disapproved and nothing came of it. He married milkmaid Patty Turner. Mainly owing to his poor mental health and alcoholism, the marriage suffered. Clare was placed in an asylum in Essex. In 1841, he escaped and walked the ninety miles back home where he imagined he would again see Mary, whom he believed was his wife. Sadly, Mary had perished in a house fire three years earlier. John Clare was committed to Northampton General Lunatic Asylum later that year, and he died there, after a stroke, in 1864.

JOHN COOPER CLARKE, the 'Bard of Salford', was born there in 1949. He worked as a laboratory technician before drifting into the Manchester folk club scene. A performance poet, he refers to himself as 'Johnny Clarke, the name behind the hairstyle'. He has appeared with the Sex Pistols, the Buzzcocks, The Fall, Elvis Costello and the Honey Monster in a Sugar Puffs ads. His poem 'Evidently Chickentown' featured in an episode of *The Sopranos*. He lives in Colchester with his wife when he's not touring.

WENDY COPE was born in Erith, Kent, in 1945. She read history at St Hilda's College, Oxford, then spent the next fifteen years teaching in primary schools. She was a TV critic for *The Spectator* and a judge for the Man Booker Prize in 2007. Her first collection of poetry sold in the thousands, and Wendy is popular with BBC Radio 4 listeners; they once voted her their choice for Poet Laureate. She was awarded the OBE in 2010.

In 2011, the British Library paid £32,000 for her entire archive of notebooks, unpublished manuscripts, scraps of paper and 40,000 emails.

EDWARD ESTLIN (E. E.) CUMMINGS was born in Cambridge, Massachusetts, in 1894. His family were strict Unitarians. At the outbreak of the First World War, he joined the army and was posted to France, where he drove an ambulance. Because of his ambivalent attitude towards Germans, he was imprisoned by the French under suspicion of espionage. Nevertheless, he developed a great affection for Paris and met Picasso there. A personal letter from President Woodrow Wilson got Cummings released. After a visit to the Soviet Union, he became an anti-Communist. Despite his easy-going manner, he was deeply conservative and an ardent supporter of Joseph McCarthy. Many of his poems were not given titles, and he rejected orthodox grammar and punctuation in favour of innovation and dynamism. His publishers often styled his name on his book covers in lowercase with no punctuation (as e e cummings). Cummings died from a stroke in 1962. He is buried at Forest Hills Cemetery, Boston.

DANTE ALIGHIERI was born in Florence, sometime around 1265. Rather than Latin, he used dialect and the vernacular in his writings to make them accessible and is often described as 'the father of the Italian language'. As a boy he saw Beatrice Portinari waving to him from a window and promptly fell in love with her. They were both nine years old at the time. Dante was exiled from Florence when he ended up on the wrong side of the long-running war between the Black and White Guelphs. Dante was White, and favoured more freedom from papal control. After wandering around Europe, Oxford included (allegedly), Dante finally settled in Ravenna. He died, it is thought from malaria, in 1321.

EMILY DICKINSON was born in Amherst, Massachusetts, in 1830. From an early age Emily was affected by what she described as 'the deepening menace of death'. Her family home overlooked the town cemetery. At times, she dressed only in white and talked to visitors from behind a closed door. She never married. Towards the end of her life Emily became a recluse. Only a handful of her poems were published in her lifetime. After collapsing while baking a cake, Dickinson died of Bright's disease in 1886. Her sister Lavinia found a locked chest full of hundreds of hand-written poems tied in neat bundles.

CAROL ANN DUFFY was born in the Gorbals, Glasgow, in 1955, to Irish parents, both of whom were working-class radicals. Her poems are widely studied in schools, although one was removed from a GCSE anthology because of a reference to a goldfish being flushed down the toilet. In 1999, Tony Blair rejected Duffy for the position of UK Poet Laureate, choosing Andrew Motion instead. But she was appointed in the role in 2009, becoming the first lesbian Scottish female holder of that post, and stood down ten years later. Dame Carol Ann Duffy has been awarded both the OBE (1995) and the CBE (2002).

THOMAS STEARNS ELIOT was born in St Louis, Missouri, in 1888. After studying at the Sorbonne, Harvard and Oxford, he settled in Britain. In 1925, he became a director in the newly formed publishing company that became Faber and Faber, where he spent his entire working life. W. H. Auden, Stephen Spender and Ted Hughes are among the dozens of famous poets he published there. He received the Nobel Prize in Literature in 1948. He married in 1957 for the second time and remained with Valerie until his death from emphysema in 1965.

ROBERT FROST was born in San Francisco, in 1874. His father died of tuberculosis when Frost was eleven and his mother from cancer fifteen years later. His personal life was beset by tragedy. Of his six children, only two outlived him. His son, Carol, committed suicide. His wife Elinor, who suffered a chronic heart condition complicated by breast cancer, died in 1938. Yet Frost wrote poetry remarkably free of self-pity. As one critic observed, 'he wrote with sympathy for others'. Frost was awarded the US Congressional Gold Medal in 1960, and his portrait appeared once on a ten-cent postage stamp. He died in Boston in 1963 after prostate surgery.

ALLEN GINSBERG was born in Newark, New Jersey, in 1926. His Jewish mother, Naomi, suffered from a number of severe mental illnesses such as paranoid delusions and spent long periods in mental institutions. His great poem, *Kaddish*, is a form of mourning for her. In San Francisco, Allen met and fell in love with Peter Orlovsky, who was to become his life-long partner. Alongside friends Jack Kerouac, Neal Cassady and William S. Burroughs, Ginsberg became a leading figure of the so-called 'Beat Movement', and his poem 'Howl' became their manifesto. He openly supported gay rights, decriminalisation of drugs and free speech. In 1968, he signed a pledge refusing to pay tax in protest against the war in Vietnam. He died in his East Village loft, in 1997, surrounded by a group of uninvited Buddhist priests chanting by his bedside and many friends, some of whom were camping there to be with him.

ROBERT VON RANKE GRAVES was born in Wimbledon, in 1895. His father was a school inspector. At Charterhouse, he was school boxing champion. When the First World War was declared, Graves enlisted immediately and wrote some of his finest work in the trenches. He was left for dead at the Battle of the Somme and suffered from shell shock. He befriended Wilfred Owen and Siegfried Sassoon, who were being treated for the same condition at Craiglockhart Hospital, Edinburgh. At the end of the war he married Nancy Nicholson, daughter of the painter Sir William Nicholson. After Graves met the poet Laura Riding, he left Nancy, and the couple went to live first in Majorca and then the USA. In 1943, Graves teamed up with Alan Hodge to write the classic guide on how to write English correctly. He then ran off with Hodge's wife, Beryl. Graves died of heart failure at his home in Majorca in 1985. Beryl shares his grave.

TONY HARRISON was born in 1937, in Leeds. His father was a baker. Harrison won a scholarship to Leeds Grammar School and later studied Classics at Leeds University. His work is political and frequently considered controversial. His long poem 'V', which was written during the minor's strike of 1984–85, is a notable example. In 2004, Harrison won the Northern Rock

Foundation Writers Award, and, in 2009, the inaugural PEN/ Pinter Prize. Harrison has been twice married and divorced. His second wife was the celebrated Greek soprano, Teresa Stratas. He lives in Newcastle upon Tyne with his partner, the actress Siân Thomas.

SEAMUS HEANEY was born in a farmhouse called Mossbawn in Tamniaran, Northern Ireland, in 1939. It features in a large number of his poems, as do his Irish origins. Heaney has won many prizes and awards: the Geoffrey Faber Memorial Prize (1968), the E. M. Forster Award (1975), the Nobel Prize in Literature (1995), Commandeur de l'Ordre des Arts et Lettres (1996), the Whitbread Book of the Year Award twice (1996 and 1999), Saoi of Aosdána (1997), the Golden Wreath of Poetry (2001), the T. S. Eliot Prize (2006) and The Griffin Trust for Excellence in Poetry's Lifetime Recognition Award (2012). He was elected Professor of Poetry at the University of Oxford (1989), named Honorary Patron of the University Philosophical Society, Trinity College, Dublin, and elected Honorary Fellow of the Royal Society of Literature in 1993. In Denmark, there is a street named after him. He died in 2013, in a Dublin hospital, survived by his wife Marie and their three children.

GEORGE HERBERT was born in Montgomery, Wales, in 1593. His father was a Member of Parliament, his mother devoted to the education and wellbeing of her ten children. He went to Trinity College, Cambridge, where he planned to study for the priesthood. But King James I persuaded him to become a politician, like his father. In 1624, Herbert became Member of Parliament for Montgomery, a job he neither liked nor felt suited for. Deeply religious, Herbert believed his calling was to serve mankind through God, not political debate. In 1630, he resigned his seat and took Holy Orders. His ministry was short-lived. Herbert contracted tuberculosis soon after he was ordained and died three years later, in 1633.

GERARD MANLEY HOPKINS was born in 1844 in Stratford, Essex. His father was the consul-general for Hawaii in London. Although he had hoped to be a painter, Hopkins studied Classics at Balliol College, Oxford. In 1877, he was ordained as a Jesuit priest. Yet he was tormented by the notion that writing poetry was at odds with devoting his life entirely to God. Hopkins caught typhoid in Dublin in 1889 and died there, a few weeks before his forty-fifth birthday. He is rightly credited with having invented modern verse. None of his poetry was published while he was alive.

HORACE was born Quintus Horace Flaccus in Venusia, in southern Italy, in 65 BC. His father had been a slave who, when made a freeman, bought land and prospered. Horace went to Athens to study at the academy founded by Plato and while there met Brutus, who gave him a job as a tribune in the army. Horace was on the losing side at the Battle of Philippi and deserted. Back in Rome he got a job as a scribe in the Treasury. He was a close friend of the Etruscan Maecenas, who introduced Horace to Augustus. Maecenas gave Horace a farm with tenants, from which Horace was able to live comfortably. Maecenas died five months after Horace in 8 BC.

ALFRED EDWARD HOUSMAN was born in 1859, in Fockbury, Worcestershire, the eldest of seven siblings. He went to Oxford in 1877, where he studied Greek and Latin. Housman fell in (unrequited) love with his room-mate, Moses Jackson. Jackson rejected Housman, but in spite of this, Jackson remained the love of Housman's life. While teaching at Cambridge, Housman had a reputation for being a savage critic, and he rarely remembered the names of his female students. His hobbies were flying, gastronomy and visits to Paris to read pornographic literature legally. He died in Cambridge in 1936.

TED HUGHES was born in Mytholmroyd, Yorkshire, in 1930. His mother's family could be traced back to William the Conqueror. Introduced to the poems of T. S. Eliot and Gerard Manley Hopkins at Mexborough Grammar School, young Ted resolved to be a poet. During his national service, he memorised vast chunks of Yeats to pass the time. He went to Cambridge to read English but found the atmosphere too stuffy, so he transferred to anthropology and archaeology. In 1956, he married Sylvia Plath. They had two children. Five years later, Hughes began an affair with Assia Wevill. Already beset with depression, Plath gassed herself. Hughes then lived with Wevill until she also killed herself. Hughes was Poet Laureate from 1984 until his death from cancer in 1998. He is honoured with a memorial in Poets' Corner, in Westminster Abbey.

CLIVE JAMES was born in Kogarth, a suburb of Sydney, Australia, in 1939. He was christened Vivian James, but his mother eventually allowed him to change his name to Clive. In the early sixties, he settled in London, where he quickly established himself as a TV critic and avuncular chat-show host. He was an outspoken atheist and a keen tango dancer. James was also an intimate of Princess Diana for a short while – 'I was enslaved,' he once wrote of her. After an eight-year-long affair with an ex-model, his wife, Cambridge scholar Prue Shaw, kicked him out. They had two children together. James was awarded an Honorary Doctorate from the University of East Anglia and was made a Member of the Order of Australia in 2003. In 2010, he was diagnosed with leukaemia. He worked harder than ever, writing essays, collections of poetry and a weekly TV column until his death in 2019.

RUDYARD KIPLING was born in Bombay, India, in 1865. When he was five, he and his sister were sent to England and Kipling was placed in foster care, in Southsea, for five miserable years, followed by boarding school. Kipling could not settle. He spent most of his life travelling, mainly between England and India. Few writers have been more prolific or popular. His *Jungle Book* and *Just So Stories* have never been out of print. Kipling was a Mason, an anti-fascist and a keen supporter of the Boy Scout movement. In 1907, he was awarded the Nobel Prize for Literature. He died of a perforated ulcer two days before King George V in 1936. He is buried in Westminster Abbey, next to Charles Dickens and Thomas Hardy.

PHILIP LARKIN was born in Coventry, in 1922. His father, Sydney, was a great admirer of the Nazi Party and attended a number of Nuremberg rallies. His son was more interested in jazz. Larkin went to Oxford to read English, where he met Kingsley Amis. They became close friends, drinking together and listening to jazz records. After a shaky start, due to a failed romance, Larkin ended up with a first-class degree. He spent most of his life working in the library at Hull University, writing poems and jazz criticism in his spare time. A heavy smoker, Philip Larkin died from cancer of the oesophagus in 1985. In 2003, he was named the nation's best-loved poet. A stone memorial in Westminster Abbey was unveiled in 2016.

AMY LOWELL was born in Brookline, Massachusetts, into a dynasty of poets, in 1874. She didn't go to college because her father thought education unsuitable for a young woman. Instead, Lowell read a lot in the family's library and collected books. She was short and stout, owing to a glandular disorder, and smoked cigars. In 1912, Lowell fell in love with Ada Dwyer Russell, who became her secretary and the subject of many romantic poems. Lowell was rumoured to have had an affair with Mercedes de Acosta, whose most famous lover was Greta Garbo. Lowell died from a cerebral haemorrhage in 1925. She was awarded the Pulitzer Prize for Poetry the following year, for *What's O'Clock*.

ROBERT TRAILL SPENCE LOWELL was born in Boston, Massachusetts, in 1917. His family were members of an upper-crust elite known as the Boston Brahmin. He was a violent bully as a child and had a very low opinion of himself; 'I am thick-witted, narcissistic, thuggish,' he once said. While at Harvard, Lowell realised he suffered from what was then known as manic depression. He was married three times and had a long affair with fellow poet

Elizabeth Bishop. He cited her as one of his major influences. Their existing letters to each other number 459. Lowell won the Pulitzer Prize for Poetry twice, in 1947 and 1974. He took lithium daily to help relieve his bipolar disorder and died of a heart attack in the back of a New York cab in 1977. He was on his way to meet an ex-wife.

ROGER McGOUGH was born in Litherland, Lancashire, in 1937. Following spells as a librarian and French teacher, Roger formed The Scaffold with John Gorman and Mike McGear (Paul McCartney's brother). In 1968, the group had a number one hit with their song, 'Lily the Pink'. In the wake of the Merseybeat phenomenon, along with fellow Liverpool poets Brian Patten and Adrian Henri, Roger published *The Mersey Sound*, an anthology of poetry that went on to sell half a million copies and become one of the best-selling poetry anthologies of all time. As well as regular radio appearances, Roger once provided the voiceover for a Waitrose TV advert. He has also translated three of Molière's most popular plays: *Tartuffe*, *The Hypochondriac* and *The Misanthrope*. He was awarded an OBE in 1997 and a CBE in 2004.

MARIANNE MOORE was born in Kirkwood, Missouri, in 1887, the daughter of an engineer who left her mother before Marianne was born. She studied history, economics and political science at Bryn Mawr College, and became a lifelong suffragist. When the family moved to New York, Marianne got a job in the public library. It was there she met Ezra Pound, with whom she had a lasting friendship. Marianne was a great sports fan, especially of boxing. Muhammad Ali was her idol, and she wrote the liner notes for his album, *I Am the Greatest!* Shortly after throwing the first pitch at the new Yankee Stadium in 1968, Marianne suffered a stroke. It was the first of many. She died in 1972.

PAUL MULDOON was born in 1951, on a farm outside The Moy, near the County Tyrone border, in Northern Ireland. Muldoon once said of The Moy, 'It's "burned into the retina", and although I haven't been back there since I left for university 30 years ago, it's the place I consider to be my home.' He now lives in New York City. He read English at Queen's University, Belfast, where Seamus Heaney was his mentor, and worked in the city as a BBC producer. Muldoon won the Pulitzer Prize for Poetry in 2003.

SYLVIA PLATH was born in Boston, Massachusetts, in 1932. Her father, Otto, was a German who wrote a book about bumblebees. While still a student, Plath had a mental breakdown and was hospitalised. She was given insulin and ECT treatment but neither was effective. This period was the inspiration for *The Bell Jar*. When Plath met the poet Robert Lowell, who suffered from bipolar disorder, he suggested that Plath wrote poems about her suicidal impulses and feelings of alienation. She took his advice. In 1956, Plath married Ted Hughes. They spent their honeymoon in Benidorm. In one suicide attempt, she crashed her car into a river. Then, in 1963, she succeeded in killing herself by putting her head in a gas oven. She was thirty.

EZRA WESTON LOOMIS POUND was born an only child in the mining town of Hailey, Idaho in 1885. He once said, 'I resolved that at 30 I would know more about poetry than any man living. I learned more or less of nine foreign languages. I read Oriental stuff in translations. I fought every university regulation and every professor who tried to make me learn anything.' After embracing fascism during the Second World War and being arraigned for treason, Pound was incarcerated in a psychiatric hospital for almost twelve years. On his release, he was diagnosed with bipolar disorder. He returned to Italy, where he died in 1972. He is buried on Isola di San Michele, an island off Venice, next to his wife Dorothy, Diaghilev and Igor Stravinsky.

LAURA RIDING was born Laura Reichenthal in New York in 1901. Her family were Austrian Jews who manufactured garments. After studying at Cornell University she met the historian Louis R. Gottschalk. They married in 1920 and divorced five years later when she met Robert Graves. In 1929, Riding survived jumping out of a fourth-floor window. Graves divorced his wife and lived with Riding – a name she invented – at his home in Majorca until the outbreak of the Spanish Civil War. After a productive creative relationship, Graves and Riding parted in 1941. She stopped writing poetry for many years. She died of heart failure in 1991.

RENÉ KARL WILHELM JOHANN JOSEF RILKE was born, an only child, in Prague in 1875. His mother, who had previously lost a daughter at birth, treated and dressed her son as if he were a girl. Aged twenty-two, he fell in love with Lou Andreas-Salomé, an older, married woman who had studied psychoanalysis with Freud.

He later married German sculptor Clara Westhoff, with whom he had a daughter, Ruth, but the marriage did not endure. During the First World War, Rilke settled in Munich, where he had a passionate love affair with the painter Lou Albert-Lasard. She was both extremely beautiful and rich. Rilke suffered from ill health his entire life. He died from leukaemia while in a Swiss sanatorium, in 1926.

CHRISTINA ROSSETTI was born in 1830, in Bloomsbury, London. Her father was an Italian political exile from Abruzzo and her mother the sister of Lord Byron's doctor. Her brother, Dante Gabriel Rossetti, was the founder of the Pre-Raphaelite Brotherhood. Christina was educated at home, spending her days reading Italian poetry. She was opposed to slavery and all forms of animal experimentation, and worked as a volunteer looking after former prostitutes. She suffered from bouts of depression throughout her life. Her poem 'In the Bleak Midwinter' was set to music by Gustav Holst. In 1894, Christina Rossetti died from breast cancer. She is buried in Highgate Cemetery.

SAINT JOHN OF THE CROSS was born Juan de Yepes Álvarez in Fontiveros, in Old Castile, Spain, in 1542. He is considered one of Spain's foremost poets. His ancestors were Jewish converts to Catholicism, and in his early twenties, he joined the Carmelites and became a very close friend of the nun Teresa of Ávila. He endured torture and imprisonment at the hands of more traditional Carmelites. Following his death in Úbeda from a painful skin infection in 1591, his body (apart from one leg) was transported to Segovia. Then it was sent back, now also minus one arm (the other had gone missing in transit). After a long dispute as to which town should have what, the Pope stepped in and declared Segovia the winner. Today, the head and torso of John are housed above a special altar.

STEVIE SMITH was born Florence Margaret Smith in Kingston upon Hull in 1902. She was nicknamed Stevie after the popular flat-race jockey, Steve Donaghue, who won the Derby six times. Stevie suffered from deep anxiety all her life. Her father, a shipping agent, abandoned the family when she was very young, and she spent three years in a sanatorium after contracting tuberculosis aged five. These events resulted in a preoccupation with thoughts of death and suicide. Sylvia Plath was a fan. Her work is sometimes thought of as childish, which is how she saw it. Stevie believed that she had a natural affinity with a child's view of the world. Her name was once romantically linked with George Orwell, although she was thought by many to be celibate. Stevie lived in the same house in Palmers Green her entire life. She died from a brain tumour in 1971.

STEPHEN HAROLD SPENDER was born in Kensington, London, in 1909. His mother was a poet and a painter. As a young man he became a committed Communist Party member. At the outbreak of the Spanish Civil War, the *Morning Star* sent him out to cover it. During the Second World War he worked for the fire service. His male lovers included Lucian Freud, and he had a six-year relationship with ex-Welsh Guardsman Tony Hyndman. He married twice, and had two children with Natasha Litvin. Their daughter, Elizabeth, is married to Barry Humphries.

Spender's brother Humphrey was a brilliant photographer. Stephen died of a heart attack in 1995.

WALLACE STEVENS was born in Reading, Pennsylvania, in 1879. His father was a wealthy lawyer who expected his son to join the family firm. Instead, young Wallace ended up in insurance. He joined the Hartford Accident and Indemnity Company, where he worked until retirement. He would concoct poetry in his head while walking to and from the office. He spent his vacations in Florida with his wife Elsie. On a visit to Key West in 1936, Stevens met Ernest Hemingway. They got into a heated argument which ended with Wallace breaking his hand on Hemingway's jaw. Stevens' work has inspired David Hockney and musicians such as Nick Cave and Vic Chestnutt. Wallace Stevens died of stomach cancer in 1955.

DYLAN THOMAS was born in Swansea, Wales, in 1914. His father said that he chose the name Dylan because it means 'son of the sea'. Thomas once said that nursery rhymes were his greatest poetic influence. He worked briefly as a reporter, and as a scriptwriter during the Second World War. Given to a life of heavy drinking and adultery, Thomas was fair game for the press, who exploited his 'boozy Welsh poet' image. However, the exposure did much to enhance his popularity. His work has been chosen no less than forty-five times by guests on *Desert Island Discs*. *Under Milk Wood* is regarded as his most outstanding work; it was performed by Richard Burton and broadcast by the BBC in January 1954, just a few weeks after Thomas' death in Greenwich Village, aged thirty-nine. In the autumn of 1953,

Thomas had flown to America for a poetry reading tour. He made a decent living there, giving lectures. While in New York, he resumed an affair with a former mistress, developed gout, and suffered from alcoholic binges, blackouts, bronchitis and emphysema. His turbulent marriage – 'the bar was our altar' – to Caitlin Macnamara is the stuff of legend. She is buried alongside him in Laugharne, Dyfed.

DEREK ALTON WALCOTT was born in 1930, on the island of Saint Lucia, in the West Indies. He studied to be a painter as a young man and loved travelling. Walcott was awarded the Nobel Prize in Literature in 1992. He married three times. In 2009, accusations of sexual harassment forced him to withdraw from the shortlist for Oxford Professor of Poetry. He died in 2017, in Saint Lucia, and was given a state funeral.

WALTER WHITMAN was born in 1819, in Huntington, Long Island. He left school aged eleven and got a job as a printer's devil before becoming first a journalist, then a poet. Ezra Pound said that Walt Whitman wasn't an American poet, he was American poetry. Whitman had intimate relationships with bus conductor Peter Doyle and Bill Duckett, among others, but he also claimed to be the father of six children. None were ever found. He loved to swim and sunbathe nude. Bram Stoker was greatly influenced by Whitman's *Leaves of Grass*, and modelled the character of Dracula on his friend. In 1940 and 2019, Whitman's portrait appeared on US Mail stamps. He died, his body riddled with abscesses and suffering from pleurisy, in 1892.

WILLIAM BUTLER YEATS was born in Sandymount, County Dublin, Ireland, in 1865. He was a poor scholar but developed a keen interest in mysticism and the occult. He proposed to Maud Gonne, for the fifth time, after her husband was executed following the Easter Rising of 1916. When Maude turned him down, he proposed to her daughter, Iseult. She also refused. In 1917, in his fifties, he married Georgie Hyde-Lees, and they had two children. A decade later, he had a successful operation to improve his sex life and enthusiastically indulged in affairs. He was awarded the Nobel Prize in Literature in 1923. Yeats died in a hotel in Roquebrune-Cap-Martin, on the French Riviera, in 1939. When his bones were transferred to Drumcliffe in Ireland, in 1948, it was discovered that they had been mixed with those of other people.

AFTERTHOUGHT

Compiling the short biographies that accompany the poems that Dorothy sent me, I was struck by the similarities. For example, the high proportion of North American poets who were born in Massachusetts to extremely wealthy and influential families. How few had needed to work for a living. I was also surprised at the number of these poets who were certifiably insane. And those who took their own lives.

In my experience, artists of all callings are often compelled to live their lives to the very extreme, especially in terms of their emotional and creative worlds. Nonconformity is their norm. It sets them apart and isolates them from the subtle support society offers when one is a part of it – a support that is not there for an outsider.

I should like to thank Professor Gilles Dupier, of L'Institut de la Reconstitution du Papier, Roubaix, and Professor Raymond Freeman of Redruth Polytechnic, who have both devoted a great deal of their time attempting to carbon-date the older manuscripts in order to authenticate them – time which sadly has yielded few, if any, positive results. Only Kipling's cigarette packet passes the test as being genuine.

I did give thought to asking those poets still living for their authentication, but I know they are busy men and women, and I suspect they would not welcome such petty intrusions into their heavy schedules. I have therefore let the matter lie.

A NOTE ON THE EDITOR

Barry Fantoni was born in London's East End in 1940. He studied painting at Camberwell School of Arts & Crafts. In 1963, he joined *Private Eye,* where he created the poet E. J. Thribb. His sixties memoir *A Whole Scene Going On* was published by Polygon in 2019. He lives in Turin.